21 Days of Jacquie

Kaylynn Zeals

India | USA | UK

Presentation by *BookLeaf Publishing*

Web: www.bookleafpub.com

E-mail: info@bookleafpub.com

ISBN: 9789363307971

First edition 2024

ACKNOWLEDGEMENT

I want to thank all those people who encouraged me to continue writing. Even when I didn't believe in myself. They knew I could do it. Thanks for the encouragement Jerrod to write my story. It's just snippets of the story, it's more to come. Kindall, Dad and my sisters for always hyping me up! Faustina Floyd for always telling me to write it down girl. I appreciate and love all the support!

PREFACE

I'm working on self care. Writing this book is a part of the process. Doing something for myself, that I genuinely enjoy doing. Every single poem is from me. How I feel and think about different topics. The more personal poems are factual. The other pieces are simply my opinion.

CONTENTS

21 Days

I write to keep my sanity. It's all only my own opinions. Do or don't take it personal. Just in my later years I felt like I'm ready to speak my voice. A voice I felt sometimes was lost in the loudness of life.

A lot of times I kept my opinions to myself. Just because I felt some type of way about a matter, don't mean I should voice my views. Especially if it has nothing to do with me.

This collection is basically 21 days of my points of view. They vary from love interest, to opening up about my personal experiences, to venting about a day at work.

I even speak on the frustrations I feel about how the world treats black people. Shelia is about a sundress. I don't even care to wear dresses! It's a few very deep personal pieces I was ready for the world to know.

When I came across this writing challenge I didn't really pay much attention to it at first. Then I seen it again and it stood out to me. It was almost like it was calling out to me.

It's about time to try my hand at this writing thing. To see where it might take me. I mean who knows, the possibilities could be endless.

So without further ado, I give you 21 Days of Jacquie.

Eve's Letter to Adam

Dear Adam,

It's me Eve. I'm sorry I've been distant for a while. I noticed my flaws and felt like you could see them too. So, I hid and avoided running into you. My low self esteem was much bolder than my full self worth. I was ashamed of what I saw and needed to go away for some time.

While I was gone, I allowed the darkness to grow deeper. It continued to spiral lower, into an intoxicating state of mind. Even on a good day I still felt ugly and was unsure of myself.

I was created from you and for you. I tarnished our connection by falling for the serpent's deceitfulness and ate the apple. I tricked you into eating it also so I wouldn't be the only one disobeying God.

Once I bit the apple it changed my way of thinking. I became unworthy in my mind. The main design of me was jaded and faded away with my insecurities that filled my brain.

I still want to be your Eve. Adam I need you to charge me up so we can procreate like it was meant to be. I apologize for damaging your rib, come help mend me back to health. You always seen the beauty in me.

Come plant your seed in my garden and we will grow our beautiful family beyond the garden of Eden. Let's walk hand and hand together into the sunset, and bond like God expected us to. Leaving behind the story of Adam and Eve; the original, He and She.

Love always, Eve

Alice L. Ballard

The heart and soul of the family. On June 15th in 1927, God created the most shiniest diamond I have ever seen in my entire life! One of the kindest, sweetest people you could have ever known.

Alice Lorine Ballard was the truth. I feel they coined the statement " kill them with kindness" around her. She had a one of a kind laugh. Just to hear it would make you laugh. Soft spoken but tough as nails. Don't get her mad, she will tell you off without using any foul language.

She lived to be around five generations in her family. Gram, you did the damn thang honey! . Everyday I think of you and miss you so very much! You definitely made my 38 years joyful here on this earth!

Now I'm watching my love go through this part of her life and it makes me sad. I can't stop the outcome! My heart breaks for her. I wish I could restore her mind to it's full capacity and stop time from moving forward.

She can recall a memory from back in the day as if it happened yesterday. But, will ask me back to back what time it is. I catch myself lashing out at the situation and it leaves a bad taste in my mouth.

I know my love ain't in her normal element. This disease don't discriminate against age, race, or color. You can tell when she's not ok, by the way her words get harsh. She is constantly going without food or sleep at times.

If you ever met her in this lifetime, you could agree that she was truly built from a different cloth. Well Gram, honey Happy 93rd Birthday my love. One day we will meet again! I love you and Rest In Peace until then.

Social Media

The Internet is one hell of a drug! Once it consumes you, it will turn you into a junkie for sure. You get to itching and fishing for likes and any kind of attention, ain't no turning back. When people call you out on it, you always deny it.

You use that famous saying; " I can stop whenever I want!" We all know it's a wrap for you. You start off by posting a few times just to get your feet wet. Then the confident status's start to roll in. You are friends with people that make you feel like a star and those likes begin to accumulate.

Which makes you seem kinda important. That amps you up a bit. You turn into a whole new you on the social sites! Dang boo, you shining, ok I see you! You have turned into a whole new you!

Getting these fake praises and likes and reinventing your life altogether. Once you finally log out and look up from behind that screen you were just glowing from. The darkness sets in and the reality hits you like a ton of bricks.

The bills are past due, the laundry is abundantly high and the dishes are never ending.

Like I said before, I see you boo. The truth isn't in the words you post. I know even when you think I don't.

Most, if not all of those "happy posts" are cries for help. I get it, to want to escape from the twist and crazy turns of your real life. Just go where the concerns and care is genuine.   Social media is very lethal.

If not handled with ease, it will destroy you and turn you into a fame monster. By the time you realize it, the damage is done and the thirst is real! Once you get hooked, your screen stays on and the new facade is there.

You can't stop lying about how things are great or how much you are in love; and want everyone to know. Then comes the tragic blow up. The internet you isn't real, and the real you is drowning in need of a life vest!

Before you know it: BOOM! Your phone is cut off and the WiFi is disconnected and you are in the real world with no bright screen to run to.

You have to face real life for a while. It's ok, just understand life is hard and overwhelming at times. Work on the real you. That fake you is only good in cyberspace.

Goodbye

That accent will get to me every single time you opened your mouth to speak. But I wouldn't say anything. I just sat back and melted on the inside. The only person so far I ever came close to loving.

I liked the person you were and that was holding me back from seeing all of your red flags. You blew your chance with me and you didn't even have a clue that I wasn't there anymore.

You understood everything you were doing to me. You pretty much figured I would always be around no matter what. It had been years since we talked. You seemed confused as to why I grew cold and heartless.

A simple text or maybe a random message once in a while, could have kept a lake warm feeling steady. Instead your selfishness made the final choice and my feelings for you were eliminated.
It took years, but I was able to let my feelings for you be gone like the wind. I didn't look back. Then years later, you pop up in town looking around for that chick you once knew.

You didn't find her. You were caught off guard from the emotionless conversation we held in my cold heartless car that night. I sat there fighting back tears and avoiding eye contact.

I didn't want to react to the face and smile, that looked the exact same as before. I wasn't done talking that night but I refused to let you see me break down.

A friend is what I was but I couldn't say the same for you. You saying sorry don't erase what happened, it only pisses me off even more. Why were you really sorry? Were you sorry that I didn't stick around? Or are you sorry that you strung me along?

I know I love hard, and my feelings were strong for you. I wonder if you were put in my shoes, what would you have done? How would you have responded to the whole situation?

I did what was best for me. That was to leave you back in Texas and move on with my life. I can say that I truly hated you without any hesitation in my voice. That hate turned into anger, which finally turned into nothing.

Why hate something that is no longer there? So I let go of all your memories and everything that reminded me of you was let go as well. Into a void of nothingness.

Stressful Day

The second half of work really stressed me out today. I completely understand that we are short staffed and I might get pulled to another location. That wasn't my issue, at all.

It's the fact that it was some unnecessary comments that was said that took me there! Then you come out into the break room and try to sound sweet and innocent like you never said anything wrong.

Well guess what? I'm the one that will go toe to toe with you, once you take me there. It will be no holds bar, uncensored round for round shenanigans and it won't be pretty. For the most part I come in to work and do my job and go home. I've seen the craziness that goes on there.

I do my best to avoid the drama at all cost. I feel that people are taking my kindness for a weakness. Once I snap on someone, they won't know what hit them. I really hate that I allowed it to bother me way after I got home.

I went to church and that helped me release some annoyance, I was still having. Now it's 8:40p.m., I'm writing about it and I still feel a type of way about the situation.

Lord please just take this from me and handle it, because I'm only human. I'm really working on myself and I want to do better. Working with ignorant people really test your character.

This type of job is so unpredictable and things constantly changes. I have to become part of the solution and not part of the problem. Today I failed the test, but tomorrow I will be more hopeful to remain positive.

Congratulations

25 years of conquering fears and shedding tears to make it to this day. This day they reconfirmed their undying love in front of all us. It all started with a broke down car and blossomed into a marvelous family.

It just continues to grow into an endless wonder. The struggles are real and with each new day their love gain more power. A man ordained through God, he leads the household as expected of him.

At first our bond was broken. However, over the years I was able to let go of others old memories. To create new ones for myself. Baby girl is my name and it takes me back to my childhood days when I hear him say it.

A woman cut from a different cloth. She shows her passion with her hands. Hands skilled to create beautiful crafts and write the most amazing poems.

Our journey started off rough as well. I wouldn't change it for the world today. I want to say I love the both of you dearly. I'm glad I was apart of your 25th year mark. I can't wait to see how many more years God will blessed your

awesome union with. I love you Jock and
Kindall Lewis!!

Martin Luther King Jr.

Martin Luther King Jr. had a dream for the human race. Not just for us black people, but for all people. He fought for equality for humans all over.

His last name alone stood for something. King: the male ruler of an independent state, especially one who inherits the position by right of birth.

We as blacks were born into royalty! Our ancestors ruled over nations. August 28, 1963 King made his dream be known all over the world. That day he commanded his audiences attention!

Whether you were right there with him or listening on the radio, or watching it on the television. You heard and felt his powerful words ring out like a siren! Martin Luther King Jr. was definitely one of our elders of the people, in his time.

He was willing to fight the good fight. This August will mark 56 years since he gave that amazing speech. Today its been 51 years since he was assassinated in Memphis, Tennessee. I'm sad to say we haven't made many strides from back then.

I mean don't get me wrong, yes things have changed. We aren't slaves to human masters anymore. We are slaves to the worldly masters. The internet and being politically correct. Not stepping on the toes of the easily offended millennials.

Don't let me get started on this so called president we have in office... GET OVER YOURSELVES! Let's come together and regain the momentum King had to win equality for the human race again!

We have let his dream fade away and become covered up by the smoke screens and the bigger picture has been lost. So let's all be more like Martin Luther King Jr. Go live out his dreams. Start demanding equality amongst us. Because deep in my heart I do believe, we too shall overcome someday!

Thank You Veterans

I want to figuratively salute you, for serving our country! That was a brave and unselfish thing for each one of you to do. I appreciate the time you put in for us. I hope your journey was well worth it for you.

Trust that God was with everyone of you the whole time. I also want to thank MY people, the true unsung heroes out there! I commend you for choosing to serve this country.

Our so called country who didn't even want to recognize you as a whole person back in the day. Still, it was ok for you to go into the service on their behalf.

Some of you really fought in the trenches. You weren't even sure if you would make it back to a safe place. Let alone making it back home to a familiar ground.

You left your families with pride and honor, and with good intentions. You were glad to go fight the good fight, some might have thought. The ones that made it back home was welcomed with cheers, happy tears and gratitude.

As those things faded away and the reality set in that you were back in the real world. I could

only imagine how it was for you to learn how to
cope after fighting a war.

PTSD, nightmares, trigger warnings by any
loud sounds. Plus way more unknown symptoms
from the affects of the atmosphere over there.
You don't know your family and they don't
know you anymore. Things are very different for
you.

The VA hospitals and benefits that should
have been readily available to each and everyone
of you, have slowly been granted to some. Once
they jumped through all the hoops and crossed
all the T's and dotted their I's. You were able to
get some relief.

This also goes out to the fallen soldiers who
are no longer on this earth, I'm sure your
memories live on with your loved ones and you
are not forgotten! I tip my hat to all of you who
took a stand to make a change. Well done
Veterans, I salute you!

Let's Fight

I call it systematic lynching! The whites are killing us at an alarming rate. And nobody is being charged with the murders. It's screwed up to say, or think that this is the new normal. We have every right to be here, just as much as YOU do.

God created all of us in his image. We are all one human race. No one race is better than the next! I'm tired and angry while I write this message. JUST STOP KILLING BLACKS!

Stop treating us like we are the problem. You're the problem, with your racist values. You come from a whole lineage of racist white people, who think they are superior to others. Well you're NOT!

Your hatefulness goes back to when you came and stole the Indian's land. Then you took the Africans from their homeland. My ancestors and brought them over here as your property.

Made them work in your fields, clean and cook in your houses, and raise your white children. Only to beat the black men and rape the black women. Who do you think you are? You are nothing but some weak minded cowards!

To hate someone because of their skin tone makes you a sick person. You only kill us and treat us like you do, because you are scared of our potential, and what we can become.

You hate because your great-great-great grand daddy told his son to hate. Each generation after continued that hate and we are extremely tired of it.

To live in America as a black person is hell on earth sometimes. To be fearful of your life when you are getting pulled over is a horrible feeling.

You instantly get a pain in your stomach and you hurry up to hit record on your cellphone. Just to make sure you have your own proof of your encounter with the law. The whole time we quietly say a prayer to God to let us make it out ALIVE!

No one should have to live like that! The police is suppose to PROTECT AND SERVE EVERYONE! That's not the case. There are racist cops out there, using the system for their own good.

Racism will continue to be in this world as long as those hateful white people continue to procreate. You can see the division of how whites and blacks are treated. Back in 2015 Dylan Roof went into a black church and killed innocent people. They brought him out in handcuffs, with a bulletproof vest on and calmly escorted him to the police car.

George Floyd was dying on the ground with a police officer's knee in his neck. He didn't even kill anyone and was treated poorly.

Even at protests you see whites with their big guns standing around and holding signs, and the cops are there keeping the peace.

When blacks protest we are unarmed holding signs, and chanting; but we get tear gas thrown at us. They are forcefully trying to shut us down! We are tired of the mistreatment of our people!

You think you get away with killing our people, when you are not convicted. The reality of it is, you didn't get away with it. God has the upper hand and you will pay for your racist acts. Trust me you didn't walk away without repercussions. You or your family will be punished for it. Trust me, it will be way more painful then the act you committed.

I believe it's going to get worse before it gets better. Racism is still alive, and it's getting bolder and bolder everyday. Black people are fed up with the racism and is already started to respond.

Some, not in a good way, with the looting and rioting. It will cause the pot to stir. There are white and black people out there peacefully protesting for the injustice of blacks to stop.

Wake up people, now is the time to change and do better! We all have rights to be treated with respect and dignity. Let's stand together and continue to fight against the unjust ways our people are being treated.

It shouldn't have to hit home to finally get a reaction out you. It's time to say enough is enough! Let's fight for all the people who died fighting for our people. Come, let's go, ITS OUR TIME NOW!

Green Grass

The grass is greener on the other side they say. Well I seen Mrs. Jones painting her lawn in the middle of the night. While Mr. Jones was creeping out the neighbors back door, zipping up his pants last night. Yet we stay trying to keep up with them. Go figure!

Mrs. Wilson's lawn is trimmed nice and neat. Probably the best looking yard in our neighborhood. Her husband passed away about a year ago. Every night she sits alone at her kitchen table, eating dinner. Her kids haven't been home in three years. Her grass looks like a picture straight from a magazine though.

The Taylor's yard is a mess. They moved into the neighborhood about seven months ago. Toys everywhere, basketball left on the porch, skates on the step. Pool noodles hanging halfway out the pool.

To look in their window they have order. Family dinners ever night. They laugh and love each other all the time. So far they only have one child, but they have discipline in their lives.

Tiffany's grass hasn't even began to grow. She has three kids by two different men. Neither one of them lends her a helping hand. Her oldest son despises her because she's too busy chasing after love to take care of her children properly. She knows she deserves better, but keep allowing the wrong men in her life.

Let me tell you about the best yard though, my yard. It has blue grass with hot pink weeds sprouting up. A bright green and orange plastic turtle sits by the front gate. He welcomes all my visitors.

Hardly any hours at work lately. Still bills are paid. It's food in the fridge. No, it's not prime rib, but it's satisfying. You see it's not about whose grass is greener. It's all about how you maintain the grass you was given.

Truckee Jay

Nineteen years ago on this day approximately 5:30pm my life changed completely. I went from thinking I was about to be set for life and make money for me and my family. To not even knowing where I was and only remembering bits and pieces of the accident.

I was still a beginner in truck driving. Only about five months out. I enjoyed driving and it was like an apartment on wheels, how exciting was that!

Let me take you back to that day. July 31, 2005 I was on my way to Maine to drop a load off. I already had a weird feeling about delivering to Maine in the first place. I had just got off the toll road and I realized I was going the wrong way.

I got off at the first exit I seen to turn around. I remember shifting then turning onto the on ramp. I felt like I was going to fast, so I down shifted and looked into my left hand rear view mirror.

It looked like my trailer was tipping over (and in my mind I'm thinking that's not happening). I look into the right hand mirror. At that point everything moved in slow motion.

I looked out the windshield and grabbed the steering wheel to brace myself, for what was about to happen. I heard a lot of noise and horns going off. Once my truck rolled and hit the ground it kept going, until the guard rail finally stopped it.

Now I'm in a panic, I tried to get up but couldn't. I wasn't even sitting in my seat anymore. I was straddling the guard rail. I hear someone yelling to see if I was ok and I say.

"I'm fine please help me out." He was shocked he said, "oh you're a woman!" I say, "yes I'm a woman please help me out of here." He said he was going to turn off the engine so nothing would catch on fire.

He runs back to his truck to call for help. I'm crying because I'm stuck and couldn't feel my lower part of my body. He comes back to wait with me until help arrives.

Paramedics get there and they are talking amongst themselves. Trying to figure out how to get me out. I'm really panicking now and I grab a water and I drink it. I ask for more water and one guy hand me a bottle. I open it and pour it on myself.

Now I see one guy motion for the others to come look. He's shining his flashlight down towards my stomach. They all come over and look in where he has his flashlight pointing. At this point I'm a crying mess.

One guy start talking to me, while he's trying to start an iv line. He tells me to talk to him. He says, "tell me about yourself." I go into telling him my name and where I live and my age.

Then I stop and ask them to please call my mom, I gave them her phone number. He puts the oxygen on me but I kept taking it off. I then tell him I was getting sleepy, he said, "just keep talking to me Jacquie."

I fade off into unconsciousness, I hear him say, "no stay awake." He sounded so far away. After that I couldn't really say what happened, or how long it took them to get me out.

I was taken to UMass Memorial Hospital and it was a blur for a lot of stuff after that. I know my mom, dad, brothers, aunts, cousins, and nephew came as soon as they could.

My whole family went through it during my accident. It didn't just change my life that day but all of our lives.

Now on this day I want to say thank you to any and everyone who helped us out during our time of need. It's so much more I want to say but I'm just going to leave this as it is.

No Worries

I'm just me and cannot and will not speak for everyone else. I can only be accountable for my actions. I sit back and watch things play out and think to myself, I guess that really happened.

At times we as people play ourselves for things we don't need but want. If I love you then why can't I be brutally honest with you and not make you feel like I'm talking down to you. Let's be real right now, the truth hurts.

This old world we live in don't give a damn if it hurt your feelings. Once that happens no one sticks around to help pick up the pieces of you, they keep it moving because it was out of spite and not love.

You see I should be able to come to you and say now you know better then that. Stop doing stupid shit. We only get mad or have hurt feelings because we know it's the truth and someone was bold enough to tell us about ourselves.

Yes please call me out on my weaknesses so I can become a better person for my future self! I want you to love me enough to tell me to wake up and realize that I'm wasting time. All my shoulda coulda and would haves are holding me back from my dreams of making it.

Learn from your past and stop using it as an excuse to become a fuck up in life. Life don't care that your dad wasn't there, or you blew that full ride scholarship to college. Use all that truth and hurt to evolve into a wonderful person and not a bitter mad at the world bum.

Everyday you wake up should allow you to change a little bit more of yourself. But hey it's ok if you don't, because I'm only talking about me right now. No worries, I love me enough to do better.

My Truth

The week after my 36th birthday, I got a call that blew my mind. It shattered me completely into a million pieces. I knew I was broken and tarnished before this and from this. But to hear what was said on the other end of the phone set my emotions array.

As I hung up the phone, I tried to sweep myself up and put the tiny pieces back together; as best as I could. The shards of me were too sharp, and only pierced me deep.

It made new cuts. As well as reopened old wounds, that were mended unhealthy to begin with. It resurfaced them as fresh as the very first time it happened.

Even though I couldn't say the first time it ever happened to me. Or why it was happening to me. The reopened wounds brought back the full weight of my pain I ever experienced.

I felt like that lonely little girl again wanting to go numb and pray it would all be over soon. Then I got pissed and embarrassed. I felt lost and unsure of myself, all simultaneously wondering why now?

Who told you it was ok to try to control me again? (but this time with the words you spoke)

In a manner that I don't like. I actually hate it! I get you want to make amends and do better for yourself. To try to build up relationships once more.

The whole situation was unsettling and just wrong. Do you know how long I waited to hear an apology? Yet it never came. It was like, it wasn't even an issue.

So, I did the best I could do for myself. I just pushed my memories down deep into a small part of me. Hoping to never have to bring them to life again. Even over the years when life felt like it was time to make me go back in.

I was strong enough to hold my composure. As of lately it has been haunting me like a never ending nightmare. It was out of my control.

At the same time it wasn't just my story. There were a few sides to be considered. I did figure one day it will be brought up to be talked about. Not only are emotions all messed up but trust was completely lost.

I guess you were trying to turn a new leaf. I'm not saying it's ok. I'm saying that God is trying to tell me, it's time to let go of some baggage. To receive new things in my life.

I'm sure I'm going to forgive but I will never forget it. The trust have been gone and I don't know if it will ever be restored. I do know that my strength is resounding and it will only improve from here on out.

Forgiveness and letting go will help my growth as a person. This has been weighing me down since I answered the phone that night. It put me in a bad place, I had never been before.

I want and need to move on from this. To allow myself to let the million pieces of me fall into the right places themselves. So I can become the best imperfect me I can be.

Brown Eyes

Her brown eyes tells her whole story. To look deep into her dark brown eyes, you will see all the pain she holds inside. Her eyes are a portal to her true self.

You could only imagine the horrors she lived through at an young age. Afraid to sleep alone at night. Dreaded staying home while her mom worked all those hours. Her innocence was taking from her, before she fully understood the meaning of the word.

Got baptized at 5 to turn into a brand new person. Only to realize nothing had changed. Finally building up the courage to tell her mom, (because she just wanted it to STOP!) for her mom to tell her: " you always telling on somebody, learn how to shut up sometimes."

She stood there lost and defeated. In that moment she had nobody on her side to save her. She learned to go numb anytime one of her three predators touched her.

She created this thick wall and vowed that no one would be worthy enough to break through. Heading to middle school unsure of herself. She met a few friends. Friends she is happy to still be friends with til this day.

Yet it was a group of kids who bullied her, for no reason. If they only knew the real her. They would embrace her and let her know it would be ok. Pushing on to high school.

She told herself she would do better with her bad attitude. A few popular guys called her a friend. They were willing to get to know her.

Now in her adult years she struggles to settle down. She pushes men away to avoid letting them in. The idea of being in a relationship sounds better than actually being in one.

She wants to do better with herself.
She's on the path of learning self care. Some things included on that path is: therapy, pedicures, movie dates, and so on. She wants people to look into her brown eyes and see the beauty that She always seen her whole life!

Inner Sanctum

I want to be right next to you and talk. Talk about your childhood dog Max, who was hit by a car on your 4th birthday. Or laughed about the silly and crazy stuff that happened to you growing up.

Our legs are intertwined together. You look over and wipe my tears. I just told you about a childhood nightmare I had, that was actually a true story.

You tell me how you're so glad I came into your life. I look so modest and unsure of what you speak of. The look you give me tells me your words you spoke are so true and sincere.

I respond to that by saying. Let's build from this bond we have. Allow it to grow into a never ending tree of creativity. I place my hand on your chest and you pull me in close to you.

I inhale your sweet smelling aroma. You smell like fresh linen and a hint of your aftershave you use. You kiss the top of my head and promise to be with me until my last dying breath.

As I lay with you, I quietly pray our days will last as long as possible. I thank God he finally put us together. I hope I will never make you mad enough to want to continue on without me in your life.

You wrap your strong arms around me and I escape into your inner sanctum for the night. Never have I imagined feeling like this, but grateful to be appreciated. In a way all women deserve to be.

Even though it hasn't happened yet I can feel you deep in my soul. I know you're out there preparing to meet me. I'm doing the same. My love keep looking for me because I'm here.

So Until Then…

I smile when I think of you. I get butterflies in my stomach, knowing I'm going to see you when I get home from work! I feel like a little kid playing with their favorite toy, every time I steal glances at you in the distance.

Every single hug and kiss brings me back to focus when I feel my mind is going crazy. That embrace heals all my woes I had for the day. It makes me ready to conquer another day.

I instantly knew you were for me because our souls connected before anything else. That feeling forced our eyes to meet. It felt like I was complete at that very moment.

I can sit and watch you play with our daughter forever. The love you give her, makes me love you even more. We speak often about having more kids and it excites my spirit.

I love how you never let me open a door we walk through. Or how you grab my hand and softly kiss it when we walk in public.

You patiently wait while I have my emotional breakdowns. After I'm done you get me right back on track, with your encouraging words.

I'm glad that I no longer fill incomplete in life. God finally put us together. The fact that I

can sit here and write this without even knowing
you yet. Tells me that I believe you are out there
and our time to meet will happen.

Belmont Pier

We meet face to face at the beach. Both times were nice. You were kind and sweet. You had a warm smile. You can tell your skin had been kissed by the sun. You had a slight golden glow to your face.

You had a nice controlled tone of voice. I felt like we had a few things in common. That made me feel comfortable with you. This is kind of weird. I like how you didn't try to hug me, you shook my hand.

Even in the moments we just sat there not saying anything was ok. The beach is my safe space. The vibes felt right but the timing was off. I was on my way back to Ohio.

We met at the end of my trip. If only we had the time, what could have been is uncertain. I definitely allowed my emotions to get the best of me. I questioned myself about being good enough.

When you brought up sex, that really over worked my mind for sure. My southern parts were one hundred percent ready. My protective walls were too strong to let you in.

I did the only thing I knew to do. That was to run away from you. I didn't want to stop talking

to you, but I also wasn't ready to go there with you.
I opened up to you about my childhood traumas and you listened quietly. You showed me empathy, in that moment I appreciated you. That was a plus in my book.

I wanted to see you again before I left. You told me it wasn't going to happen. I went back home with hurt feelings and regret. I didn't take the time to really express my feelings properly.

I don't know what the reason for our meeting was, but it made me realize something about myself. I needed to work on some unresolved issues within me. To become better for myself. I do hope we get to meet face to face again. When I'm in a better state of mind. I can show you the healed version of myself.

Happiness

I just want to be happy. I honestly can't say what that looks like though. I remember my brother asking me if I ever been happy in life. To look back I can say I've had happy moments. But, I've never been just happy with my life. He held me and cried.

What would my happiness look like? I can't imagine it for real. I can say I would be an entrepreneur, doing my baking. I would be the boss, running my own business.

Definitely writing more books. Whether it's for myself, or ghost writing for someone else. I could see myself writing for tv shows. I could picture me doing that. I get happy just thinking about baking and writing.

To hear people say they like my material is my happy place. My happiness don't have to be a thing, a feeling is good enough to me. To watch someone's facial expressions as they bite into my desserts makes me happy.

To hear someone talk about how they liked a poem I wrote. One guy was so excited after I performed a poem. He said you described sex while using an instrument and making music at the same time! Then he said, "can you send that to me?"

I get happy butterflies in my stomach. All those times were happy moments. I'm in search of my happiness now days. It's time for me to be happy. So if you see me out in public alone and I seem to be enjoying myself. Mind your business; ok?

Happiness is whatever we want it to be. I know it's simple. I know I will figure it out soon. Once I reach that element I can see more layers of my protective wall melt away. I will connect with myself at a new deeper level.

I will not let anybody take this feeling away from me, no matter what. It took me too long to reach this point in life. Now go find your own happiness; and leave mine alone.

My mom

Girl you look just like your momma. I'm not gone mess with her, that's Kay's daughter. You have to be a Ballard, because you look just like them. I've heard this all my live. It never gets old.

I get happy to hear people say I look like my mom. Or to hear them say, I knew Kay, she was crazy. I'd smile and agree with them. Carolyn Kay Ballard was definitely a beautiful soul.

It's been over eight years since God called you home. I miss you EVERYDAY! Im getting teary eyed writing this right now. Im so glad I had you for 34 years!

You told me this a few times; God knew to only give me one daughter. Was I that bad mom? Im so sorry for the attitudes and mood swings. At times I was just a bitch, for no reason.

Our relationship with truly a rollercoaster ride of emotions. I wouldn't trade you for any other mom out there though. You were the one for me. Now being grown and thinking back you did your best.

I remember coming across your old pay stubs. You were only making $6.50, all while raising four kids! That wasn't enough, but you worked it out. We always had what we needed! Sometimes we got what we wanted as well.

Man mom I want to make you proud of me! You would always say you were proud of me. I never felt worthy. Now I'm taking risk and working harder then ever. I love you and keep watching over me. At times I feel you right by my side. Rest in peace my love.

Shelia

Yesterday morning I woke up to a nice breeze across my shoulder blades. When I turned over, the sun slowly met my face with a warm kiss. It made me feel loved. I laid there for a minute to take it all in.

I opened my eyes and smiled because I knew what kind of day it would be for me. Today I had a few errands to run. I might as well do some retail therapy while I'm out. I had the perfect thing to wear!

I got up, yelled to Alexa to "play my morning mix." Then proceeded to the bathroom. First song to play was Miss Corrine Bailey Rae; Put your records on. I turned the water on in the shower and shimmied out my pjs, down to my birthday suit.

I loved to feel the water hit my face, to fully awaken my whole entire soul. I continued my daily bathroom routine. I headed back to my room to get dressed. I stood in front of my mirror and dropped my robe.

I looked into the mirror and admired what I saw. ALL OF WHAT I SAW! My hips, dips, curves, dimples, pimples, scars, bumps and bruises. Yep, it's all me. I flashed my beautiful smile and threw myself a wink and moved on to my rub down portion of my morning.

Now that I'm smelling good and feeling amazing, I put on my unmentionables first. Then I went to the closet to find Shelia. Oh, Shelia is my favorite sundress. YES; I sure did name her!

I raked through my clothes looking for her. I saw her and get excited! I found her last year at this cute little boutique on my vacation. I slipped her over my head and slid her down my body.

She hugged my body like she hadn't seen me in forever! I stepped back and pranced in front of my mirror. I said, "Yasss Shelia, you better show off my cake honey!"

I did a quick messy bun with my dreads, picked up my shades off the dresser and put on my sandals. I got my keys, and out the door I went. I was ready to show off Miss Shelia in that awesome sunny day.

She and the sun were dance partners that day, let me tell you! Shelia twirled and swished in the breeze all day long. I just knew I was looking good that day.

As I strutted through town I enjoyed my time out. I would smile and give a head nod to the others passing by. In my head I was thinking: "Man, Shelia is giving me life right now!"

Once I made it home, I sat on my couch feeling accomplished. I got my errands done,

and found a few good treasures on sale. Today
was a Sunday, funday in my beautiful Shelia!